DON'T FEAR
FIGHT

*The 7 Spirits That Are
Attacking Women Today*

DR. RENA PEROZICH

DON'T FEAR FIGHT

The 7 Spirits That Are Attacking Women Today
By Rena Perozich

ISBN: 979-8-9917173-9-7

Prepared for Publication By

B B

PUBLISHING

MAKING YOUR BOOK A REALITY

Cedar Point, NC | 843-929-8768
BandBpublishingLLC.com
info@BandBpublishingLLC.com

CONTENTS

Thank You

I want to thank God for never leaving me to myself. He has never abandoned me. I give Him all the credit for this revelation and warning to the Body of Christ. It is His desire that no one should perish.

First, I want to thank my husband of 48 years for always believing in my prophetic gift, and for drawing on it in ways that have strengthened and sharpened the anointing on my life as a Prophet.

I also want to thank Pastor Deborah Swecker and the Women of Witness, who first heard this message and encouraged me to write it down so it could be shared. My prayer is that you hear the Holy Spirit speak to you personally through this revelation, and that you respond with wisdom to protect yourself, those you love, and those you are called to serve.

Thank you to all who read and re-read this message to help with edits and corrections. You know who you are—and how much I love and appreciate each of you. May God richly reward you.

And thank you to B&B Publishing for never rushing me, but allowing God to ferment this message in my soul until its due season.

DON'T FEAR: FIGHT

*This know also, that in the last days peril-
ous times shall come.*

2 Timothy 3:1 KJV

*"You emphatically must know what I am telling you!
In the very last part of the last days, in the very end
of the age, hurtful, dangerous, unpredictable, uncontrollable high-risk periods of time will come."* - **As stated in
Sparkling Gems by Rick Renner.**

God shared with me all that I am sharing with you
in the book you hold in your hand. These spirits will
be unleashed upon the earth to assassinate women—
to kill suddenly or secretively, murder premeditatedly
and treacherously. These are released upon the earth to
destroy or harm us viciously. They are not from God,
they are from the enemy of our being—the devil. God

wants His women armed and ready to do warfare. This information is to inoculate you.

Many of these spirits I have seen come upon the earth over the last five years. I feel a strong urgency to get this book out to women across the nation. Help me share the word of the Lord, so that we can protect ourselves. We must understand the signs of the times to prepare ourselves, our sisters, and our daughters for what is coming.

This is a book of transition. No matter where you find yourself, know that there is an enemy that seeks to destroy women. Why? They are His secret weapons. God has always used women since the beginning of time. He used women when He sent His Son to the earth the first time, and He will do it again. You, reading this—you are His weapon of warfare.

Introduction

The problem with many of us is we have been satisfied with the handfuls that everyone else leaves behind. We don't say it like that. We say it like this, "Well, that is the way it is in the workforce: women make less money than men for doing the same job. All the women in our family have been abused. Divorce runs in my family. Weight loss is too difficult for the women in my family. We all have tempers. We are a hard-headed bunch..." We identify with our past and live defeated in our present. God is calling for us to come apart from our yesterdays, and venture into a new field and find what He has for us.

We are praying too small, because we are thinking too small. We pray for more straw so we can make more bricks when God wants us to live as free women, not slaves. His desire for us is to possess the land, not to work ourselves to death. God's desire is not for us to live on leftovers.

We think if we are thin enough, we will be beautiful. We compare ourselves with models that we can never look like, rather than embrace our individual body type. We try fad diets that are insufficient, poorly balanced, causing faulty digestion and utilization of the foods we consume, causing premature death.

The book of Ruth is a symbolic book. The characters take us from what was, to what is to be. Situations and circumstances changed both Ruth and Naomi. Situations and circumstances change all of us. They both needed to move beyond their past to reach their destiny. So do we and together we can help one another. However, in these last days, there are spirits unleashed against women. The book you hold in your hand was from a visitation I had from God. He shared with me this message and told me that as women, we must protect ourselves from these spirits; that the information could inoculate us and protect us from being assassinated by the devil. I am sure this little book will be highly controversial. I may be ridiculed and even attacked. Knowing this, I share what I have received as a great privilege. It was not on my agenda, but I laid aside my agenda to do His will.

"On the other side of obedience is the blessing."
- Joe Perozich

Chapter 1

DEADLY DESIRES

Deadly desires are just that, things that we desire that are deadly.

We desire what we don't need. We make ourselves miserable trying to provide ourselves with things that can't make us love ourselves, better ourselves, or solve our problems. If we are married, we might make our husbands feel pressured to provide, or, worse yet, give up trying to provide. Why? Because the lies of the enemy tell us, "Not enough education, not skinny enough, I'm not enough." God wants you to know you are enough. He is enough. God has all things and if you seek Him, you will lack no good thing. Seeking Him, not things, is the solution to all our desires.

Deadly desires drive us. Jesus leads us. Deadly desires cause us to live a dissatisfied life. We become miserable and make everyone around us miserable. Desires that drive us ultimately destroy us. We work too hard and seek Him too little.

Time is approaching for Jesus' return and the devil wants to take us out when we are most needed. Boaz has his eye on us. We are not a breed of Naomis, but a new breed of Ruths. We can serve our way to success. We may have come from a terrible background, but we must refuse to let our history determine our destiny.

Here, right where you are, God is forming your character in your field of dreams. This is where the enemy sows seeds of deadly desires.

Where are these deadly desires coming from? On Demand? Livestreaming? Social media? Television? Podcast? Wherever these seeds of desire are coming from, stop them now. Those seeds will determine what you birth. Ruth made a decision to serve, and she focused on that one thing. In so doing, she birthed what she was. She gave birth to Obed, whose name literally means servant. Obed was the father of Jesse, who was the father of David and from that kingly line came Jesus, the greatest servant of all.

Women, the enemy of our soul wants us to fail in birthing significant seed. The enemy wants to determine our harvest. If we are filled with selfish, deadly desires, that is what we will birth. We can only bring forth what is inside of us. What we attach ourselves to matters. What we give ourselves to will control us. What we compromise to keep, we will lose.

When Ruth gave birth, it turned Naomi's clock back and her old leathery breast filled with milk enough to nurse Obed. God will bless us until we will not have room enough to contain it if we will refuse to become bitter. God is faithful. Desire Him and He will give you the desires of your heart. Try to help someone unselfishly and see what God will do.

You might be reading this full of desire for things. You may feel empty. You have lived and lost. You have loved and lost. You may have left your past and lost. But God is in the business of finding what is lost. He wants to give you the desires of your heart, but only if those desires are in line with His will for your life. God is not willing to give us anything that cost us our relationship with Him. He wants us more than anything. He wants you and He is not willing to lose you to deadly desires.

God wants us to enjoy our food. God wants us to live long and live strong. He wants us to have nice things. He wants you to feel beautiful, dress beautifully, and be adorned with grace. He rejoices in the prosperity of His saints.

QUESTIONS

1. What is your heart's desire?
2. What do you want more than anything?
3. How are you willing to compromise to get what you want?
4. Do you want what you want, more than you want to give God what He wants?
5. Where are your desires coming from?
6. Who or what is feeding that desire?

God is the answer. He is always the answer. Starve your cravings and deadly desires. Feed instead on dying to self and giving God what He wants. After all, we have been bought at a price. Our bodies are not our own once we are saved. The great exchange has taken place.

> *"For you were bought at a price; therefore, glorify God in your body and in your spirit, which are God's."*
> ***1 Corinthians 6:20 NKJV***

NOTES

NOTES

Chapter 2

WORKING OURSELVES TO DEATH

The deceitfulness of riches added to the desires for other things will choke the word of God out of our life. When this happens, we become unfruitful. Barrenness is on the rise here in the United States of America. More women are in the work field than ever before. We, along with our spouses if we are married, have often got caught up in the lie that both husband and wife must work to survive. We have forgotten about Jehovah Jireh, our provider.

> *"and the cares of this world, the deceitfulness of riches, and the desires for other things entering in choke the word, and it becomes unfruitful."*
> **Mark 4:9 NKJV**

We work so we can have, but too often find ourselves too tired to enjoy the fruits of our labor. Rather than share the burden with our children and teach them to help with family chores and the value of money, we spoil them and try to give them everything we didn't have when we were growing up. In my experience of over thirty years sharing with mothers, I have concluded; your children are not little versions of you, and they don't want what you wanted. It would surprise parents to know what their children really want. Ask them! Often, a child will choose time with their parents, over stuff from their parents.

The devil works to bring disorder. Anything out of order will bring pain. When the family system is out of order, everyone suffers. Just like if a bone is out of place, or a spine is out of alignment, there will be pain—there will be additional damage. The enemy will try to pervert what God's plan and purposes are for our life and family. When children learn at an early age that a family requires everyone to give, take, share, and do their part, they make much better adults. Life will not be a rude awakening for them or overwhelming because they naturally grew into becoming a servant and are now celebrated adults; that can find and keep a job. They can enter relationships knowing that for it to work, there is always give and take, not just take.

In referring to the Book of Ruth, when we find ourselves in the right field, we make the right connections. We get paid more than we could imagine. Ruth's reputation preceded her. She was known for what she did at home. She was known for serving. We do not have to work ourselves to death. Connections matter. Where you go to church matters. The Lord knows what we have need of. When God knows what we need, He provides. All we need to do is trust and obey. Ask Him according to His word. If we ask for a piece of bread, He will not give us a stone.

> "Or what man is there among you who, if his son asks for bread, will give him a stone? 10 Or if he asks for a fish, will he give him a serpent? 11 If you then, being evil, know how to give good gifts to your children, how much more will your Father who is in heaven give good things to those who ask Him! 12 Therefore, whatever you want men to do to you, do also to them, for this is the Law and the Prophets."
> **Matthew 7:9-12 NKJV**

> "Therefore do not be like them. For your

Father knows the things you have need of
before you ask Him."
Matthew 6:8 NKJV

"So why do you worry about clothing?
Consider the lilies of the field, how they
grow: they neither toil nor spin."
Matthew 6:28 NKJV

Women, we were made to be a helpmeet for our Adam, not all Adams (Genesis 2:18). We were made to bring forth the desires of God on this earth. A woman was the first evangelist for Jesus. He met her at the well (John 4:4-26). She wasn't living the life she should have been living, but one encounter with Jesus changed her forever. Esther saved a nation (Esther 8-9). She was a single, orphaned woman raised by her uncle. God didn't care. He needed her to deliver His people. We never see where Deborah was married, yet she served as the Judge of a nation and won battles (Judges 4). Jael knew how to use her female charms and a tent peg (Judges 4:21). Rahab the Harlot knew how to use information and what was hers and saved herself and her household (Joshua 2). We do not have to work ourselves to death we just need to do what God is calling us to do.

QUESTIONS

1. What has God called you to do?
2. Is He asking something of you right now?
3. Where in your walk have you said, "No"?
4. What has God asked you to lay aside or walk away from?

Harden not your heart. The more we say no, the easier it is to say it again and again. Keep a tender heart toward God. Read in His word about how much He loves you. God doesn't want something from us. He wants to get something to us. All He requires is that we love Him and have no other gods before Him.

"I am the Lord your God, who brought you out of the land of Egypt, out of the house of bondage. You shall have no other gods before Me."

Exodus 20:2-3 NKJV

NOTES

Chapter 3

SELF-HATRED

Hating our self is not of God. God gave His Son to die for us. God loves us. We are to love what God loves and hate what God hates.

Comparing ourselves with others is not wise. We often hate ourselves only compared to what we see in others or perceive about others. Often, what is on the outside is not what is on the inside. Looks are deceiving.

> "For we dare not class ourselves or compare ourselves with those who commend themselves. But they, measuring themselves by themselves, and comparing themselves among themselves, are not wise."
> **2 Corinthians 10:12 NKJV**

Jesus saved us. Jesus freed us. We are a new creation. We are all called to be fishers of men-not fisherman (fisherwoman).

We are not called just to catch people in our net of dysfunction and keep them captive by our harsh words, to control or manipulate. We are made to be containers of LOVE. God is love and His desire is to live inside of us and manifest Himself through us to others.

We are called to love ourselves. Only when we love ourselves can we ever hope to love others. If we fail to love ourselves and instead loathe ourselves, we will always use and abuse others to make ourselves look good. People full of hate hold themselves to an ungodly standard and then measure others by that same standard. It is a self-isolating behavior. No one wants to be around someone hateful—full of hate.

There is a saying, "If Momma ain't happy, ain't nobody happy." Not sure who coined the phrase, but it's a truism. I learned from an early age a mother's attitude can change the face of the world, at least for the world of her children. A man does not want to marry an unhappy woman. It is not a man's job to make a woman happy. Joy comes from the Lord. The joy of the Lord is our strength. If you want to love yourself, you must first fall in love with the lover of your soul—the one who gave His life for you.

You are fearfully and wonderfully made.

> *"I will praise You, for I am fearfully and wonderfully made; Marvelous are Your works, and that my soul knows very well."*
> **Psalm 139:14 NKJV**

Our soul is our mind, our will, and our emotions. Those three areas give us a lot of trouble. If we can convince those parts of us, the rest of our being will follow. Joyce Meyer was right in her book, The Battlefield of the Mind. Our mind is truly where the battle is. Ladies, when we bring our mind under submission, the body will follow. The mind will cause us to see ourselves differently. God may wash our eyes with tears as Ira Stanphill penned, but we will see much better. We will see through the eyes of love.

> *"You shall not take vengeance, nor bear any grudge against the children of your people, but you shall love your neighbor as yourself: I am the Lord."*
> **Leviticus 19:18 NKJV**

You are beautiful. There is no one like you. Making others small does not make us bigger. The Bible tells us that our worth is more precious than rubies and nothing can be compared to us.

"She is more precious than rubies, and all the things you may desire cannot compare with her."

Proverbs 3:15 NKJV

"Judge not, that you be not judged. 2 For with what judgment you judge, you will be judged; and with the measure you use, it will be measured back to you. 3 And why do you look at the speck in your brother's eye, but do not consider the plank in your own eye?"

Matthew 7:1-3 NKJV

"Don't run up debts, except for the huge debt of love you owe each other. When you love others, you complete what the law has been after all along. The law code— don't sleep with another person's spouse, don't take someone's life, don't take what isn't yours, don't always be wanting what

you don't have, and any other 'don't' you
can think of—finally adds up to this: Love
other people as well as you do yourself.
You can't go wrong when you love others.
When you add up everything in the law
code, the total is love."

Romans 13:9-10 MSG

QUESTIONS

1. Do you love yourself?
2. Do you have difficulty loving others?
3. Why do you feel unworthy of love?
4. Do you know for certainty God loves you?

If you answered, "No." Where in your life's journey did you lose the love for yourself?

When the man dropped the axe head, he ran and told the man of God and the man of God asks him, "Where did you drop it?" Then, he took him back to where he lost it. The man of God then threw a stick in the water and the axe head came up and floated.

"And the sons of the prophets said to Elisha,
"See now, the place where we dwell with
you is too small for us. Please, let us go to
the Jordan, and let every man take a beam
from there, and let us make there a place

where we may dwell." So, he answered,
"Go. "Then one said, "Please consent to go
with your servants." And he answered, "I
will go. "So, he went with them. And when
they came to the Jordan, they cut down
trees. But as one was cutting down a tree,
the iron ax head fell into the water; and
he cried out and said, "Alas, master! For it
was borrowed. "So, the man of God said,
"Where did it fall?" And he showed him
the place. So, he cut off a stick, and threw
it in there; and he made the iron float.
Therefore, he said, "Pick it up for yourself."
So, he reached out his hand and took it."
2 Kings 6:1-7 NKJV

Sometimes we have to go back to where we lost a thing. Perhaps it was your innocence, purity, or free loving, childlike spirit? Whatever it was, however you lost it—go back and find it again. The tree that Christ was crucified upon holds a promise that what dies can live again and what was once lost can be found.

NOTES

NOTES

Chapter 4

SOWING SEEDS OF DISCORD

Toxic emotions are just that: toxic. Strife, dispute, war, lack of harmony between people can kill us. The devil would love for us to disagree and clash with our sisters and brothers. Why? Because together we are better.

When someone starts in on a conversation that you know full well is not in harmony with the word of God, get out. The devil always brings division. God always brings unity. The Lord hates many things, but one of the big ones is sowing discord. When we bring division, we are being used by the devil. Refuse to allow yourself to be sucked into this trap. Stop up your ears. Refuse to be a trash can. Mark the person and move on. Do not make a habit of being the "go-to" for sister trash mouth. Remember, we are to keep our vessels pure and uncontaminated.

When you begin to feel division and discord, this is the time to address it. Asking questions for clarification can go a long way. Have I offended you? I feel there is something between us. Do you feel it as well? Sometimes, simply an apology or expressing your desire to improve a relationship can make a big difference.

Ruth had to learn to be a part of the gleaning team. Even though Naomi stopped speaking to her, Ruth continued to press in to Naomi. Harmony in the relationship benefitted them both. It is the same in family and in church, two are better than one. If we have ought against another person, we are to go to them directly, not everyone else but them.

"Two are better than one, because they have a good reward for their labor. 10 For if they fall, one will lift up his companion. But woe to him who is alone when he falls, for he has no one to help him up. 11 Again, if two lie down together, they will keep warm; but how can one be warm alone? 12 Though one may be overpowered by another, two can withstand him. And a threefold cord is not quickly broken."
Ecclesiastes 4:9-12 NKJV

"Do not nurse hatred in your heart for any of your relatives. Confront people directly so you will not be held guilty for their sin."
Leviticus 19:17 NLT

"You're familiar with the old written law, 'Love your friend,' and its unwritten companion, 'Hate your enemy.' I'm challenging that. I'm telling you to love your enemies. Let them bring out the best in you, not the worst. When someone gives you a hard time, respond with the supple moves of prayer, for then you are working out of your true selves, your God-created selves. This is what God does. He gives his best— the sun to warm and the rain to nourish— to everyone, regardless: the good and bad, the nice and nasty. If all you do is love the lovable, do you expect a bonus? Anybody can do that. If you simply say hello to those who greet you, do you expect a medal? Any run-of-the-mill sinner does that."

Matthew 5:43-47 MSG

QUESTIONS

1. Am I being used as an instrument of harmony or discord?
2. Before we open our mouths to speak, we should ask ourselves, "Would I want this said about me?"
3. Am I being used by the enemy in my conversations?
4. "Is this what love would say?" If the answer is no, then ask the Lord to help you. He is as close as the mention of His name.

> "The Lord is near to all who call upon Him, to all who call upon Him in truth. 19 He will fulfill the desire of those who fear Him; He also will hear their cry and save them."
>
> **Psalm 145:18-19 NKJV**

NOTES

NOTES

Chapter 5

MURDER

There are many definitions of murder. One definition that the Lord spoke of when He gave me this revelation five years ago was abortion. For many states, it was legal according to the law of the land, but never by the Creator of the land and Giver of Life. Murder is the killing of one human by another, especially with premeditated malice. It means to put to an end, to destroy.

Seeds of murder are often planted because of an offense. When that seed matures, it is proof of what it contains, such as bitterness or rage.

"Just before the Passover Feast, Jesus knew that the time had come to leave this world to go to the Father. Having loved his dear companions, he continued to love them right to the end. It was suppertime. The

Devil by now had Judas, son of Simon the Iscariot, firmly in his grip, all set for the betrayal."

John 13: 1-2 MSG

Satan knows how to lure people into situations where they feel hurt and offended. Then, he coaxes us into nurturing our offense until it mutates into strife that separates family, friends, and churches. The devil will wait and watch us for opportune times, just like it takes a while for a seed to bloom and bear fruit. He will prey on us when we are weary, tired, hungry, and not feeling well. When someone says or does something that we cannot understand, or it triggers an old wound, thats the time he injects a fiery dart of offense into our emotions. If we are not aware of this, we allow bitterness to take root and permit division to mount up in our hearts. This can grow into full bloom murder.

Satan found a way to enter into Judas.

"Six days before Passover, Jesus entered Bethany where Lazarus, so recently raised from the dead, was living. Lazarus and his sisters invited Jesus to dinner at their home. Martha served. Lazarus was one of those sitting at the table with them. Mary

came in with a jar of very expensive aro-
matic oils, anointed and massaged Jesus'
feet, and then wiped them with her hair.
The fragrance of the oils filled the house.
4-6 Judas Iscariot, one of his disciples, even
then getting ready to betray him, said,
"Why wasn't this oil sold and the money
given to the poor? It would have easily
brought three hundred silver pieces." He
said this not because he cared two cents
about the poor but because he was a thief.
He was in charge of their common funds,
but also embezzled them. 7-8 Jesus said,
"Let her alone. She's anticipating and hon-
oring the day of my burial. You always
have the poor with you. You don't always
have me."
                                    John 12:1-8 MSG

"And supper being ended, the devil hav-
ing already put it into the heart of Judas
Iscariot, Simon's son, to betray Him,"
                                    John 13:2 NKJV

Money is often used by the devil to bring offense.
I believe a seed was planted; a fiery dart was thrown
into Judas's heart when he got offended over the spike-
nard.

Where did that thought originate? It didn't come from God. Any killing, destroying, or stealing comes from the devil himself. Our goal is to have on our shield of faith that will deflect every fiery dart.

QUESTIONS

1. So, think about that. When did Satan put this into Judas's heart?
2. Has Satan ever cast anything into your heart?
3. Have you ever felt a desire to harm someone?
4. Are you easily offended? If so, in what area?

> *"above all, taking the shield of faith with which, you will be able to quench all the fiery darts of the wicked one."*
> **Ephesians 6:16 NKJV**

NOTES

NOTES

NOTES

Chapter 6

MISDIAGNOSIS MALADIES

We could define this as misdiagnosis malady or any disorder or disease of the body, especially a chronic or deep-seated spirit of infirmity. A spirit that cannot be diagnosed. An infirmity that seems to move, hide, and not be confirmed with diagnostic testing and does not respond to medication or treatment.

In these last days, the devil will try to put anything and everything upon women to hinder them from fulfilling their call. These evil spirits will try to deceive many into believing they are sick, old, and weak, when in reality it is an onslaught of lying spirits. Lying spirits will try to throw the doctors off from properly diagnosing God's people.

If you are feeling sick and the medical field cannot find anything wrong with you, it may be this spirit. I once was sick for nine months and had spent over 10,000 dollars (my deductible). My condition was worsening. In desperation, I went to my pastor one last time. I was losing hope. My pastor prayed and said, "I believe this is a spirit of infirmity." He prayed against that spirit. The next day was Sunday, and while I was singing the spirit left me. It has never returned.

Tell yourself the truth. You are healed, and the devil is trying to make you sick. Refuse to agree with the diagnosis and rebuke the symptoms. Take good care of your body, as it is the Temple of the Living God.

"Now a certain woman had a flow of blood for twelve years, 26 and had suffered many things from many physicians. She had spent all that she had and was no better, but rather grew worse. 27 When she heard about Jesus, she came behind Him in the crowd and touched His garment. 28 For she said, 'If only I may touch His clothes, I shall be made well.' 29 Immediately, the fountain of her blood was dried up, and she felt in her body that she was healed of the affliction. 30 And Jesus, immediately knowing in Himself that power had gone out of Him, turned around in the crowd and said, 'Who touched My clothes?' 31 But

His disciples said to Him, 'You see the multitude thronging You, and You say, 'Who touched Me?' 32 And He looked around to see her who had done this thing. 33 But the woman, fearing and trembling, knowing what had happened to her, came and fell down before Him and told Him the whole truth. 34 And He said to her, 'Daughter, your faith has made you well. Go in peace, and be healed of your affliction."

Mark 5:25-34 NKJV

Her faith made her whole. Now is the time to increase our faith. Faith comes by hearing and hearing the Word of God. Take time every day to get into the Word of God, and not just get into the Bible but allow the Bible to get into you. They are words of life to us and health to our (flesh) bodies.

"So you shall serve the Lord your God, and He will bless your bread and your water. And I will take sickness away from the midst of you."

Exodus 23:25 NKJV

"The spirit of a man will sustain him in

sickness, but who can bear a broken spirit?"

Proverbs 18:14 NKJV

A healthy spirit can conquer adversity. Yes, adversity will come, but it cannot overcome.

"that it might be fulfilled which was spoken by Isaiah the prophet, saying: He Himself took our infirmities and bore our sicknesses."

Matthew 8:17 NKJV

QUESTIONS

1. Do I have a healthy, balanced diet?
2. Is my lifestyle healthy?
3. Do I speak well of myself?
4. Have I ever used my words against me? Such as "My back is killing me. I hate my legs. I wish I were dead."
5. When I have a symptom, do I immediately go into fear mode and think thoughts such as, "I probably have cancer. This runs in my family. I need to see a doctor. Etc."
6. What am I doing to keep my spirit man healthy?
7. Do I take a Sabbath?
8. Do I occasionally fast?

NOTES

NOTES

Chapter 7

VAST ATROCITIES

Every day in the news we can read about some shocking and cruel event. An atrocity is a ferocious and appalling action. Such as a woman driving through an intersection at over a hundred miles an hour, killing many in her wake, people shooting into schools, crowds, theaters, and malls.

We have seen bombs placed along the finish line of marathons, killing people and wounding hundreds of people. Events that come to mind are the Holocaust, the Armenian genocide, World Wars, earthquakes, rioting in the streets, the events of 9/11, just to name a few. But, in these last days there will be more events and of a higher magnitude than we have seen. We will see vicious, wild and uncontrollable people acting as animals, unpredictable and dangerous. Many of these will be targeted explicitly against women.

I share these not to bring fear upon us as women but to alert us to the times in which we are living and the warfare that we are to endure and to overcome.

> *"They landed in the country of the Gadarenes and were met by two madmen, victims of demons, coming out of the cemetery. The men had terrorized the region for so long that no one considered it safe to walk down that stretch of road anymore. Seeing Jesus, the madmen screamed out, 'What business do you have giving us a hard time? You're the Son of God! You weren't supposed to show up here yet!' Off in the distance, a herd of pigs was grazing and rooting. The evil spirits begged Jesus, "If you kick us out of these men, let us live in the pigs."*
>
> **Matthew 8:28-31 MSG**

> *"For God has not given us a spirit of fear, but of power and of love and of a sound mind."*
>
> **2 Timothy 1:7 NKJV**

> *"You are of God, little children, and have*

overcome them, because He who is in you
is greater than he who is in the world."

1 John 4:4 NKJV

"No weapon formed against you shall prosper, And every tongue which rises against
you in judgment You shall condemn. This
is the heritage of the servants of the Lord,
and their righteousness is from Me, says
the Lord."

Isaiah 54:17 NKJV

QUESTIONS

1. Do you believe God orders your steps?
2. Do you agree with the Word of God that says God has a future of good prepared for you?
3. Will God give His angels charge over you?
4. Do you believe no weapon formed against you will prosper?
5. Are you living in fear? If so, of what?
6. Are you secure that Jesus loves you and promises good to you?
7. Are you strong in the belief that God will protect and care for you? If the answer is yes, that's great—go share your faith with others. But, if the answer is no—run to the Father. Tell Him your concerns and ask Him to replace your fears with confident assurance that He is with you and will never leave you.

"And the LORD, He is the One who goes before you. He will be with you, He will not leave you nor forsake you; do not fear nor be dismayed."
Deuteronomy 31:8 NKJV

NOTES

NOTES

NOTES

Conclusion

All these spirits I have discussed are loose upon the earth to assassinate women—to kill suddenly or secretively, to murder premeditatedly and treacherously. They are from Satan, the enemy of our soul. But, praise God for greater is He that is in us than he that is in the world (1 John 4:4).

> *"Here are six things God hates, and one more that he loathes with a passion: eyes that are arrogant, a tongue that lies, hands that murder the innocent, a heart that hatches evil plots, feet that race down a wicked track, a mouth that lies under oath, a troublemaker in the family."*
> **Proverbs 6:16-19 MSG**

We can see from this passage of scripture that God hates these six things. These six things are all included in the message God gave me in this dream that I have just shared with you.

GUARD YOURSELF

In the Amplified Bible version of this verse, we can find ourselves guilty on many accounts. God is not mocked. He knows us. He sees us. He forgives us when we repent. But, we must not just turn from sin; we need to go in a different direction—Gods direction.

> "These six things the Lord hates; Indeed, seven are repulsive to Him: 17 A proud look [the attitude that makes one overestimate oneself and discount others], a lying tongue, And hands that shed innocent blood, 18 A heart that creates wicked plans, Feet that run swiftly to evil, 19 A false witness who breathes out lies (even half-truths), And one who spreads discord (rumors) among brothers."
>
> **Proverbs 6:16-19 AMP**

Satan is a deceiver, and he desires to destroy us. He always tries to pervert what God does. We must guard ourselves and never put our desires over the desires of the Lord. Eve desired what the Lord forbid. Her decision still affects us today.

Who will your decisions affect? What has God told you not to touch, eat, do, say? Scripture tells us that

Eve was deceived. We can be easily deceived when we want what we want, more than we want what God wants.

> *"Then the Lord God said to the woman, 'What is this that you have done?' And the woman said, "The serpent beguiled and deceived me, and I ate..."*
> **Genesis 3:13 AMP**

The Word of God is our weapon, and it will keep us from being beguiled, cheated, outwitted, and deceived. However, it cannot override our own free will. You and I must heed the Word of God.

I believe that in sharing this, you have been inoculated with protection against the devil's weapons. However, just like any other inoculation, our body must still fight against the intruder, the trespasser. Our weapons are not carnal but mighty.

> *"For the weapons of our warfare are not carnal but mighty in God for pulling down strongholds,"*
> **2 Corinthians 10:4 NKJV**

WE MUST REPENT TO RECEIVE REVELATION

Ask God to forgive you for coming into agreement with any of these assignments. Don't allow your history to determine your destiny.

You are a woman of God, and this is your time. We become like those who we spend time with. Gather yourself with other women, who are of like precious faith, ready to be a weapon in the hand of God against these 7 Spirits assigned to assassinate women.

Can you be today's Ruth? Today's Esther? Today's Deborah? Today's Jael? I believe you are.

ACTION STEPS

The questions at the end of each chapter can be used as a devotional, Small Group, or Bible Study.

- I welcome feedback on these 7 Spirits by contacting me on my website at **renaperozich.com**

- Share this book with a friend.

- Buy a copy for someone else and sow it into their life. Many do not know who they are, and so they will allow others to put a label on them that God did not intend.

- If you do not know that you have an enemy, you will not be prepared to fight. God wants His women prepared for the battle that is about to take place.

- Take your place on the battlefield. God will protect you.

- Find a church that preaches the gospel. Once you find one, get involved.

- Read your Bible.

- Pray in the Spirit. (An excellent book to help you with this is Praying in Tongues is Normal by Teresa Verdecchio, available on Amazon)

- Pray the prayers at the end of this book.

- Be aware of your surroundings. Stay under cover of your parents if single, your husband if married, and regardless of your situation, married, single, divorced, or widowed stay under the covering of your pastor.

- Often, we open ourselves to these spirits because of trauma, childhood emotional neglect, abandonment, or other unfortunate circumstances, and happenings. If you need a coach to help you sort through these, go to **renaperozich.com** to book a session with me. Allow me to help you or refer you to someone who can. We all see life through different lenses. Perhaps we just need our lenses cleaned? I know I did.

PRAYER

Father, protect me from these spirits sent to assassinate me, my sisters, my daughters, my granddaughters, my mother, my aunts, my friends, and all women of God who call upon your name.

CONFESSIONS

1. **I come against the spirit of "Deadly Desires."** You are my protector. I submit myself to you, Lord. I take heed of this warning and will arm myself with the Word of God and all humility. I desire You above all things, people, and pleasures the world offers.

2. **I come against the spirit of "Working to Death".** I will not work myself to death. I will work six days and remember the Sabbath. I will remind myself and renew my mind that sufficient

for the day are the cares, and that You care for me. You clothe the lilies and feed the sparrows, and I know You will care for me. You will clothe me and provide for me.

3. **I come against the spirit of "Self-hatred."** I love myself. I am not rejected because You accept me. I am not less than because You live inside of me and You are all I will ever need. You made me. You gave me life. You died for me. You are for me, not against me. I am fearfully and wonderfully made. I am the apple of Your eye. I am precious in Your sight. I am forgiven. I am made whole.

4. **I come against the spirit of "Sowing seeds of discord."** I refuse to sow discord in my family, on the job, in my church, and among my friends. I vow to live in harmony with the Body of Christ and to be an example of a godly woman in the world. I will put a watch guard on my mouth. I will think on things that are true, noble, right, pure, lovely, and admirable — if anything is excellent or praiseworthy that is what I will focus on. I am forgiving and loving. I am a peacemaker. I will not take part in gossip or speak evil.

5. **I come against the spirit of "Murder."** I love

life. I am a life giver, not a life taker. Forgive me for ever taking part or participating in all murderous acts. (If applicable—Forgive me for having an abortion/abortions. I receive your forgiveness. Forgive me for talking other women into having an abortion or funding an abortion.) I pray for all women everywhere who find themselves pregnant with nowhere to turn. Lord, use me to help and love others. Keep me free from all bitterness, envy, strife, jealousy, and murderous thoughts and words in Jesus' Name.

6. **I come against the spirit of "Misdiagnosed Maladies."** I refuse to agree with any symptoms that come against my body, my mind and/or my emotions. My first line of defense will be the Word of God. I will speak to my body and tell it what the Word says. I will find out in my Bible if I don't know what the Word says. I will ask my pastor to help me. (An excellent resource is How to Live and Not Die by Norval Hayes. If you cannot find it, don't hesitate to contact our ministry through restorationchurchintl.org and we will help you get a copy.) I will not accept an evil report as the gospel. I will get a second opinion. A bad report is not the final say. God has the final say. I will pray the prayer of faith. I will call for the church's

elders to pray and anoint me with oil. I will fast. I will speak to my body and tell it to be made well. I will command symptoms to go! I will live and not die.

7. **I come against the spirit of "Vast Atrocities."** I will stay submitted to the authorities in my life. I will stay out of strife, for where there is strife, there is every evil thing. I will know my surroundings and make wise decisions. I will avoid being in the company of fools. I will ask my covering and the intercessors of my local church to cover me in prayer when I travel and minister, when I am on assignment or travel to the mission field. I will wear the armor of God mentioned in Ephesians 6. I will be sensitive to the voice of the Holy Spirit to lead and guide me. I command angels to go before me and be on my rear guard. I plead the blood of Jesus over me.

AUTHOR'S CLOSING NOTE

I sincerely pray that you will fulfill your God-given call, and be safe in the days ahead. I am expecting these prayers and confessions to strengthen and empower you. God loves you. He believes in you. Now, believe in yourself and be the weapon He has called you to be. DON'T FEAR: FIGHT!!! You are exactly what God needs in this hour.

NOTES

ABOUT THE AUTHOR

Dr. Rena Perozich is a pastor, prophetic voice, and founder of Women of Witness, a multi-denominational ministry empowering women to discover their God-given purpose. With a ministry footprint in over 20 nations, Dr. Rena is known for her healing, deliverance, and bold biblical teaching.

She co-hosts the Christian television program Believe Right with her husband and mentors believers in faith, identity, and spiritual warfare.

Her writing equips readers to live victorious, fear-free lives anchored in God's truth.

Learn more at **renaperozich.com**.

www.ingramcontent.com/pod-product-compliance
Lightning Source LLC
Chambersburg PA
CBHW071348130626
46556CB00005B/2078